JESUS,
FRIEND
of My
SOUL

"Joyce Rupp has given us a treasure not just for the days of Lent but for all our days. The treasure is right in the title: *Friend*. As we walk her reflections, we meet Jesus as our friend, and day by day, as we fall more in love with his tender compassion, we begin to realize that he is calling us to be a friend as he was a friend to the whole world."

Janet Conner
Creator of the *Praying at the Speed of Love* podcast

"In *Jesus, Friend of My Soul*, Joyce Rupp invites us to walk with Jesus as our soulmate. Each day we reflect on a quality of Jesus that is illustrated by scripture and pray on that quality with Rupp's poetic and beautiful, image-filled prayers. These daily Lenten reflections and their call to act on Jesus' qualities will help you embrace Christ-like virtues and live in a grace-filled way."

Terry Rickard, O.P.
President of RENEW International

"Lent has never been my favorite time of year, but Joyce Rupp makes the season a joyful adventure. She has reintroduced me to Jesus—a longtime friend whom I am able to see now with new eyes—and identifies simple yet profound ways I can model qualities of his life in my own. I love who I might become this Lent with this book in hand."

Ann M. Garrido
Associate Professor of Homiletics
Aquinas Institute of Theology

"Rich and enriching, *Jesus, Friend of My Soul* provides us with a beautiful companion for our journey through Lent: Jesus himself. With a generous heart and a keen eye, Joyce Rupp finds ways of connecting Christ to our own lives, reminding us of his humanity and message of boundless hope. Insightful, inspiring, and lit by joy, *Jesus, Friend of My Soul* offers us a new way to mark the days leading up to Easter and leaves our hearts uplifted for the days that follow."

Deacon Greg Kandra
Award-winning journalist and blogger at *The Deacon's Bench*

JESUS, FRIEND
of My
SOUL

REFLECTIONS *for the* LENTEN JOURNEY

JOYCE RUPP

AVE MARIA PRESS AVE Notre Dame, Indiana

Founded in 1865, Ave Maria Press is a ministry of the United States Province of Holy Cross.

www.avemariapress.com

Paperback: ISBN-13 978-1-59471-965-3

E-book: ISBN-13 978-1-59471-966-0

Cover image © gettyimages, Philippe Sainte-Laudy Photography.

Cover and text design by Brian C. Conley.

Printed and bound in the United States of America.

Library of Congress Cataloging-in-Publication Data
Names: Rupp, Joyce, author.
Title: Jesus, friend of my soul : reflections for the Lenten journey / Joyce Rupp.
Description: Notre Dame, Indiana : Ave Maria Press, 2020. | Includes bibliographical references. | Summary: "In each two-page daily reflection of this book, Joyce Rupp brings the reader's attention to the Lenten season, providing reflections for growth and inviting the reader to follow Jesus and become more like him"-- Provided by publisher.
Identifiers: LCCN 2019046025 (print) | LCCN 2019046026 (ebook) | ISBN 9781594719653 (paperback) | ISBN 9781594719660 (ebook)
Subjects: LCSH: Lent--Prayers and devotions. | Jesus Christ--Example--Prayers and devotions. | Bible. Gospels--Devotional use.
Classification: LCC BV85 .R87 2020 (print) | LCC BV85 (ebook) | DDC 242/.34--dc23
LC record available at https://lccn.loc.gov/2019046025
LC ebook record available at https://lccn.loc.gov/2019046026

CONTENTS

INTRODUCTION

Unlike Mary of Magdala peering into the empty tomb on Easter Sunday morning, I stood looking into my niece's chicken coop with its small flock of clucking hens. The Alleluias of the Easter Vigil from the previous evening sang in my soul as the sight before me awakened the memory of a familiar scene long ago. I saw myself as an eight-year-old girl with the job of feeding chickens on the farm. With a bucket of oats and cracked corn in hand, I carried on a one-way conversation with my friend, Jesus, whom my teacher in the three-room schoolhouse introduced as a trusted confidante. Without a murmur of resistance, my young soul sipped in that teacher's enthusiasm for this beloved companion.

Seven decades later, I look back on that child with awe and gratitude. The sense I had then of a holy presence and the assuredness of a steadfast mentor of spiritual kinship remain with me to this day. Although my forms of prayer change with age and images of divinity increasingly blur, the goodness of Jesus continues as a central inspiration for how I live.

What would we observe had we been walking with Jesus as he moved among the people of his time? We can, in a certain sense, do this by "walking through" the gospels. When we read attentively, we catch sight of who he is, how he responds to others, and what he teaches about living in a grace-filled way. St. Symeon, an eleventh-century theologian, refers to Jesus' humanity in this way: "The formless and invisible God, without change or alteration, assumed a human form and showed himself to be a normal human being. He ate, he drank, he slept, he sweated, and he grew weary. He did everything other people do, except that he did not sin."[1] The traits of Jesus' divinity reside within his human existence. Noted author Frederick Buechner emphasizes, "You glimpse the mark of his face in the faces of everyone who ever looked toward him or away from him, which means finally of course that you glimpse the mark of him also in your own face."[2]

The Qualities of Jesus

To be a Christian includes more than memorizing prayers and reciting religious creeds. First and foremost, Christian identity requires having the marks of Jesus influence our hearts and the way we live. As Christians, we look to the person of Jesus to learn from him. This involves coming to know his essential goodness by continually returning to what he taught and how he lived. His goodness is to be a pattern for our own behavior. Celtic poet John O'Donohue remarks in *Walking in Wonder* that we are each "the custodian of an inner world," one that "other people glimpse . . .

from the way we behave."[3] With few exceptions, the most difficult task of a Christian involves that of being a living exemplar and conduit of Christlike virtues.

Because my life, like most people's, fills to the brim with too much activity, my ability to express Jesus' qualities can wane and even slip away from me entirely. And so, each year when Lent arrives, I step into the season with a desire to restore and enliven my relationship with the One who is central in my heart. The noble aspects of Jesus call me home with restored encouragement (and inevitable challenge) to have those features of goodness more fully revealed through my personhood and daily living.

In *Jesus, Friend of My Soul*, an inspiring attribute from the life and teachings of Jesus is presented each Lenten day. We ponder this quality as Jesus lived it and look to see how this characteristic comes alive in us as we go about our daily activities. By doing this, we gradually become more attuned to living these virtues.

Time and again the gospel writers describe crowds of people eager to see and meet Jesus. They come for a variety of reasons. Some are merely curious. Others long for some part of themselves, body or spirit, to be healed. Many are drawn to his preaching. What they discover is that they receive more than what they came for: the curious are invited to come closer; those with physical ailments have their faith strengthened; the ones hoping to lessen inner woundedness hear affirmation for their courage; and some listeners are so inspired that they leave all and pledge their lives to his path.

What will it be like for you this Lent? What and whom will you seek? Like the people of Jesus' time, you may well receive something different or more than you expect if you spend time with him. As you pray with these qualities of Jesus, you might discover that some of these virtues limp along in your life and could use some enlivening, while others move with a steady, positive activation.

The goal of *Jesus, Friend of My Soul*, is best expressed with the following statement of Beatrice Bruteau in *The Easter Mysteries*: "We are following Jesus as our archetype, as well as our teacher and our friend, the one who exemplifies the very transformation we are facing. . . . We are going deeply into ourselves, dying to our former way of seeing, feeling, thinking, acting, in order to discover our secret self and be reborn into a new way of seeing, feeling, thinking, acting; and we are going deeply into Jesus, the exemplar, as he invites us deeper and deeper into himself as the Living Way."[4]

There it is. The path has been prepared for a Lenten walk. Will you take a step each day and arrive at the door of Easter with a more expansive love for Jesus? Will you accept the opportunity to receive renewed inspiration and have a more solid determination to be a tangible carrier of his teachings? I join you in spiritual kinship as we move ever closer to the heart of Christianity, to a more complete expression of the qualities of Jesus, who is our Living Way.

Ash Wednesday to First Sunday of Lent

ONE WHO INVITES

He said to them, "Come and see." They came and saw where he was staying, and they remained with him that day.

—John 1:39

What a difference there is between being obligated to attend a gathering and being free to decline. There is also a difference between a gathering that takes place at a public domain and one within a home environment in which getting acquainted develops more easily. The disciples expressed curiosity about Jesus. He suggested they meet where he was staying so they could get to know him. Where did this revealing conversation take place, and what did they see? Scripture does not give us the particulars of what these seekers experienced. But something truly significant occurred during the time they spent with Jesus. When they left that dwelling place, the hearts of these inquisitive visitors glowed.

They desired to commit their future to this man whose spiritual magnetism drew them to him.

A similar, heartfelt response to "come and see" awaits us during this Lent. By spending time with the qualities of Jesus, we are able to be more intimately acquainted with his personal traits of goodness. We do so by going to where his Spirit stays—in the home of our hearts and in the larger dwelling place of the world. As our hearts ignite with a renewed desire to give ourselves more totally to the abiding love of Jesus, we become credible invitations for others to come and see this divine Companion who enthralls us with his beloved presence.

Mentor of my life,
I stand at the threshold of the Lenten journey,
knowing I have the ability to learn from you.
I can accept or decline your open invitation
to abide attentively in your dwelling place.
I desire to set my heart on belonging to you.

Today: I accept the invitation to "come and see."

ONE WHO IS DISCIPLINED

If any want to become my followers, let them deny themselves and take up their cross daily and follow me.

—Luke 9:23

There were undoubtedly moments when Jesus wanted to return to Nazareth and lead a quiet, unencumbered life in which no one pestered him for help. The days of crowds with hurting people steadily pressing upon him, the times his disciples failed to perceive his message, or the moments when skeptics openly taunted him about his beliefs—these were surely tough times for Jesus. Yet he persisted in being there for others. He welcomed those in distress. He continued to love his disciples. And he never gave up on teaching. His journey required a lot of prayer and disciplined willpower for Jesus to live a life of unconditional love.

And so, too, with our lives. Some of our situations include tough things we have to bear, even when we do not want to do so. It takes much discipline and courage to enter into what we are unable to shove out of the way. Our troubles and crosses are unique to each of us. They might come in the form of old hurts, persistent addictions, financial problems, relationship struggles, physical or mental illness, undesirable duties, or the constant grayness of grief and depression. Like Jesus, when certain aspects of life cannot be altered, we accept them as sources of spiritual transformation, trusting that qualities such as resilience, compassion, patience, and kindness will mature in us.

Bearer of the Cross,
no one wants to have burdens and afflictions,
yet they come into our lives and weigh us down.
I can learn from you how to shoulder my troubles
and find my greatest source of strength in you.
Help me to deny myself when it is required.

Today: I choose to accept the cross of my difficulties.

ONE WHO PRAYS

In the morning, while it was still very dark, he got up and went out to a deserted place, and there he prayed.

—Mark 1:35

In the midst of intense work, Jesus left the constant demands on his presence and went to be alone with his most cherished confidante. There he found necessary restoration. Did Jesus hesitate to care for his weariness, knowing there was still much to be done? If he was fully human, this tension probably existed for him, as it does for us when work or other happenings keep piling up with little relief in sight. The gospel writers seldom tell us what or how Jesus prayed. They only reveal that he deliberately placed himself apart to commune with his heart's first love. His vibrant ministry gives ample evidence of the reinspired stimulus he gained during these solitary sojourns.

We learn from Jesus that we need to be faithful to our inner life if we are to remain motivated in giving the best of ourselves to others. I think of this when I want to get on with the day's pressing activities and omit morning meditation. It's not so much about *what* or *how* we pray as it is the fact that we purposefully pause to strengthen the bond of our connection with the Holy One. Let us put aside our electronic devices, TV programs, constant work, or whatever else lures us long enough to go apart and spend some quiet moments with the One who sustains our relationship.

Intimate Confidante,
you know how much I value your presence.
You also understand when I do not follow through
with my intention to strengthen our relationship.
Keep drawing me to your compassionate heart
until I readily give my time to refocus and renew.

Today: I step aside to pause and enter a quality
time of prayer.

ONE WHO SEES GOOD IN OTHERS

He looked up and said to him, "Zacchaeus, hurry and come down; for I must stay at your house to-day."

—Luke 19:5

What would you do if someone with a reputation for being no good showed up in your life? Would you want to spend time with him or her? That is exactly what Jesus did. His open-minded, inner vision peered beneath the layers of cheating and dishonesty in Zacchaeus and discerned something valuable within him. Not that Jesus denied the reality of the man's immoral behavior. Instead, Jesus chose to focus on the goodness residing within Zacchaeus. He trusted the man's potential to change.

Do we give people a second chance when they've hurt us? Do we pigeon-hole them into categories, believing they'll never be different? Does a voice in our heads say such things as "That guy won't amount to anything" or "She's always been that irresponsible"? I look back to when I was young and see how people took a risk by inviting me to develop my talents when they were submerged under a veneer of criticism and mistrust. When I remember this, I deliberately concentrate on the latent virtues in others. While abuse and harmful behavior are never acceptable, we can allow people the opportunity to amend their ways. Everyone fails. Everyone contains a basic core of goodness. Let's look for that, as Jesus did, and invite those who offend us by their attitudes and behavior to have another chance.

Deep-Seeing One,
you know my wrongdoings and limitations
and are also well aware of my essential goodness.
You value in me what I do not always see.
Help me believe in my virtues and good qualities.
Remind me often to give others a chance to grow.

Today: I give thanks for those who trusted my latent virtues.

First Week of Lent

ONE WHO CHOOSES WISELY

Jesus, full of the Holy Spirit . . . was led by the Spirit in the wilderness. . . . Then Jesus, filled with the power of the Spirit, returned to Galilee.

—Luke 4:1, 14

Who of us has not been tempted away from what is good? The opposing forces we encounter vary, depending on our personalities, lifestyles, and careers. These choices include taking the easy way out or choosing the more difficult path that involves our responsibility, opening our mouths or keeping them shut, walling off our hearts or taking the bricks down, fighting and resisting or trying to make peace, running away or remaining in a tough commitment, and turning away or turning toward those who suffer unfairness. These and many other choices are ours to make. Jesus faced his own choices and decisions, particularly during those forty days when he experienced his temptations. Out of that struggle, with the Spirit's assistance, the integrity of Jesus remained intact. He chose to go forth to his ministry as a humble servant, one who would go so far as even to wash the dirt-encrusted, smelly feet of his disciples.

Perhaps the most important message of the time Jesus spent in the wilderness is that he was *led in* by the Spirit and *led out* by the Spirit. When we face daunting alternatives that lead to either drawing forth our goodness or hiding it further, beneficial assistance arrives when we pray to the Spirit for guidance and choose to do what aligns with the teachings of Jesus.

Guiding Spirit,
when opposing forces in me tug and pull
and I am caught in the tension of choices,
nudge me to pay attention and to pray.
I trust that you will continually lead me
to make wise decisions toward what is good.

Today: I make decisions that come from my best self.

ONE WHO LETS GO

Unless a grain of wheat falls into the earth and dies, it remains just a single grain; but if it dies, it bears much fruit.

—John 12:24

A seed contains an amazing potential for life. Before this growth can take place, the seed gives way for its hard outer layer to split apart. This allows for the life inside to awaken and sprout. Jesus knew what it was like to be a seed. Throughout his life, he had to relinquish good things in order to bear fruit. He left behind a secure life in Nazareth to be faithful to his mission. He let go of being understood and of receiving acceptance from the people in his hometown, and he released any hope he may have had for a good reputation among the religious leaders. Each time his teachings and activities were disregarded, challenged, or rejected, Jesus let more of the seed's husk fall away. Jesus did not turn his back on what he felt called to be and do. His life bore fruit because he continuously gave open-heartedly of himself.

Challenging circumstances generate opportunities for the seed of divine life in us to grow. Whenever a situation summons us to open ourselves more fully, we become like the wheat grain Jesus described. Major loss, failure, disappointment, illness, discontent—things of this nature lead us to discover facets of life-giving goodness in ourselves, but only if we are willing to release what holds us back and keeps our inner shell from softening.

Surrendered One,
I am the seed in the hiddenness of the soil.
The thick covering that I try hard to preserve
seems to take forever to release and open.
Keep softening that hard-shelled part of me
with your encouragement for my ability to grow.

Today: I nudge the seed in me to open further.

ONE WHO GRIEVES

Jesus began to weep.

—John 11:35

Jesus stood by the tomb of his beloved friend Lazarus. His friend's sister Mary came and knelt before him, weeping. Jesus felt her sorrow and became "greatly disturbed in spirit and deeply moved" (Jn 11:33). His tears flowed from his loss and joined hers in empathy. What was it like for this mentor with a torn heart to stand in front of everyone and cry? Did he feel humbled because he couldn't appear strong and stoical? Apparently not. He allowed his sorrow to be both felt and observed. Jesus did not feign false control. In *The Wild Edge of Sorrow*, Francis Weller wisely describes "grief work" as a process that takes courage and "deepens our connection with soul."[1] When Jesus stood before the tomb of Lazarus and wept, he allowed the emotional part of himself to be touched by that death. As we allow tears to rise from our broken-open hearts, we enter a healing realm for the aching loss that stretches far inside of us.

Grieving is a healthy, human response to the pain of no longer having someone or something significant. Weeping does not indicate a lack of faith. There is nothing unholy about having a good cry to express our sorrow. When we grieve, we show tenderness for our broken heart. This virtue aids our healing process. As we weep, we also unite compassionately with others whose shattered hearts fill the world with endless tears.

Restorer of broken hearts,
when sorrow empties joy from my life
and situations bring unforeseen bleakness,
wrap your arms of tender hope
around the wounded edges of my hurt.
Urge my grief to move toward healing.

Today: I entrust my wounded heart to the divine Healer.

ONE WHO ENJOYS LIFE

> There was a wedding in Cana. . . . Jesus and his disciples had also been invited.
>
> —John 2:1–2

We are given little information about the hidden life of Jesus—how he lived or what he did during his years at Nazareth before he left home for his public ministry. There is another hiddenness about his life: the gospels supply almost no details about what brought Jesus pleasure. With a few exceptions, such as his presence at the Cana wedding, we miss knowing what caused him to laugh, how he appreciated delightful moments, or when he felt especially contented. We can be fairly confident that enjoyable experiences occurred if he was fully human, but we must read between the lines to notice how they happened. I can imagine Jesus at the wedding happily greeting others, joining in the dancing, thoroughly engaged in the joyous event. Jesus also observed the natural world, evidently taking pleasure in it because he often referred to nature in his teachings and parables. When he held children with their wonder-filled eyes, they surely captured his heart.

Sometimes we take ourselves, and even the spiritual realm, too seriously. Our intensity develops into a lifeless approach in which we miss enjoyable opportunities; but experiencing those opportunities is an essential component for a healthy inner life. When we become overly intense about who we are or how we intend our spiritualty to be, it is time to lighten up, to notice the incongruity and craziness that exists. A good laugh (especially at ourselves) can ease the intensity and help us to be reenthused.

Enchanter of my heart,
even during the disciplined Lenten season
there will be opportunities to take delight
in little joys strewn throughout the day.
Unseal my overly serious self
so I will enjoy the pleasures coming my way.

Today: I appreciate something that brings me gladness.

ONE WHO
LIVES KINDLY

In everything do to others as you would have them
do to you.

—Matthew 7:12

This attitude applies to *all* of our life—every thought,
word, and deed of ours that connects us to others in
some way. How would we feel if our thoughts, words,
and deeds regarding others came back to us in the same
form? I cringe at the implication. When I am careful
to treat others as I want to be treated, kindheartedness
underscores everything I think, speak, and do. This attitude is not sugary and showy but consists of having a
basic respect for each individual.

Kindness begins in the mind. How we think about
others precedes how we act toward them. Condescen-
sion, jealousy, racial profiling, arrogant dismissal—
much of these stem from a perception regarding the

worth of another person. Would we want certain people to judge us the way we evaluate them? How much harsher our assessments of others can be than our assessments of ourselves. We excuse, tolerate, or understand our less-than-satisfactory behavior because of family history, stress, illness, or simple forgetfulness, but we may not give others these same allowances. We require them to measure up to our expectations and conform to our firm standards. Jesus treated people kindly, especially those deemed unworthy by social, religious, and political criteria. He allowed for cultural and personality variances and approached these differences with an openness that every one of us relishes when we receive this type of response.

Kindhearted Teacher,
I desire to be rid of negative judgments.
May every thought, word, and deed of mine
be grounded in respect for self and others.
I pray that I will approach and act toward each
person with a kindness that reflects your response.

Today: I approach each person as worthy of respectful kindness.

ONE WHO RECONCILES

First be reconciled to your brother or sister, and then come and offer your gift.

—Matthew 5:24

When it comes to rifts in human relationships, life was not all that different in the time of Jesus than it is in ours. People who came to him with their troubles most assuredly talked about the burden of injured feelings and the alienation existing between relatives and friends. Descriptions of who did what to whom would have arisen, along with stories of quarrels and questions of how to possibly rebuild what had been ripped apart.

Merriam-Webster's Dictionary defines *reconcile* this way: "to restore to friendship or harmony."[2] *Restoring friendship* does not come easily for most. Not for me. I want the one who hurt me to admit it and express regret. I do not want to be the first to step toward the other. However, reconciliation does not work that way. The heart clothed in love seeks to find a way to restore harmony with the other person. Like Jesus going to Peter after Peter's appalling denial of knowing him, we can take the first step. Jesus did not wait for Peter to say he was sorry. Peter never left his heart, and Jesus wanted him to know that. He restored the relationship and welcomed Peter's return with the vital question: "Do you love me?" Peter's response—"You know that I love you"—closed the chasm between them (Jn 21:15). It solidified a relationship that lasted a lifetime.

Divine Reconciler,
strengthen me when I take that shaky first step
of opening my heart to someone who has hurt me
and bravely begin the process of closing the chasm.
May my heart be big enough to set aside differences
and bring back harmony into valued relationships.

Today: I take another step toward reconciling
with someone.

ONE WHO IS A FRIEND

Jesus loved Martha and her sister and Lazarus.

—John 11:5

To have a friend and be a friend—it's such a supportive, rewarding gift. Imagine being with Jesus in the house at Bethany where his friends Martha, Mary, and Lazarus lived. Luke tells us that Martha opened her home to him (see Lk 10:38). These friends welcomed Jesus and provided a space for him where he didn't have to be concerned about the crowds demanding his attention. There he could relax and be at ease due to their generous hospitality, whether engaged in conversation, quietly relaxing, or sharing a meal.

Some years ago I experienced having the best friend I had ever known. Then he suddenly died. Every day I am grateful for what he taught me by his Christlike qualities—especially how to live with a kind heart and generous spirit. I often wonder how he put up with my foibles and goofiness. Being a faithful friend can be taxing. People disappoint. They sometimes fail to hear what is expressed. Jesus remained friends with his disciples even though they often "didn't get it" and even when they lacked courage to be with him in his worst anguish. Although they did not always return his friendship, Jesus consistently invested his love in these relationships. He assured them, "I have called you friends, because I have made known to you everything that I have heard from my Father" (Jn 15:15). Jesus extends the same gift of friendship to us and invites us to share it with others.

Friend of my soul,
you dwell in the innermost part of my heart
and continually support our relationship.
Your hospitable presence awaits my welcome
when I pause to communicate with you.
The gift of your friendship sustains my life.

Today: I recognize the value of friendship and
give thanks.

SECOND WEEK
OF LENT

ONE WHO IS BELOVED

And a voice came from heaven, "You are my Son, the Beloved; with you I am well pleased."

—Mark 1:11

When I began leading Boundless Compassion retreats, I was surprised that the most challenging day for the majority of retreatants centered on the topic of compassion for one's self. I learned that a lot of people do not feel worthy of either God's love or their own. Thus, they do much better at offering compassion to others than to themselves, often putting their own needs as the last to be tended. When they accept that they are "a beloved" like Jesus, they can more readily be kind to themselves. Scripture assures us that every human being is made in the image and likeness of the Holy One (see Gn 1:27), that we are held in love by this divine Being like parents who "lift infants to their cheeks" (Hos 11:4).

During the baptism of Jesus by his cousin John, Jesus heard clearly how fully he was cherished. "This is my Son, the Beloved," announced and confirmed the intimate and lasting bond Jesus experienced with the Holy One whom he called *Abba*, Father. This message must have carried both consolation and motivation as Jesus went about his often grueling and intense work. He recognized his worthiness and approached others with knowledge of their own belovedness. Are we aware that we are cherished by the Creator? Do we find comfort and strength in this reality as we go about our daily tasks?

Beloved One,
how wondrous a gift to be forever loved,
for you to extend a wide welcome to me.
When I hesitate to believe in this reality,
steer my misgivings toward your assurance
and hold me close to your all-embracing heart.

Today: I ponder the wonder and truth of being
beloved.

ONE WHO EXTENDS MERCY

Be merciful, just as your Father is merciful.

—Luke 6:36

An elderly sister in my community sat on the edge of her bed. That day she was to move from a spacious room where she resided for two decades into a tight, narrow room in a health-care area. I was assigned to assist with the packing. I knew she dreaded the process. As I stood in the doorway, I observed the emotional struggle on her face and the way her shoulders drooped in resignation. Before entering, I prayed to be as kind as possible, remembering how harshly this woman treated me years earlier. I searched my heart and felt only compassion for what this sister was going through. I wanted her to be at peace. When I arrived home that evening, I understood more clearly what mercy entails.

This virtue lived in the heart of Jesus. He certainly had reason to admonish repentant Peter for his blatant denial, but he did not do this. Instead, Jesus approached him with a merciful welcome and assured Peter that the past need not overshadow the future. Strong emotions such as anger and bitterness can deter us when someone asks for our forgiveness. If we do not tend to these emotions, they develop into strong barriers, keeping us from giving the requested pardon. When we meet the painful past and choose to put it behind us, we are ready to offer mercy to those who have offended us.

Bountiful Love,
may your astounding mercy go forth from me
whenever I encounter injurious situations
in which I can choose to release someone.
Let me not forget or quickly set aside memories
of when your mercy freed my own soul's burden.

Today: I carry gratitude for divine mercy given to me.

ONE WHO IS HUMBLE

Learn from me; for I am gentle and humble in heart.

—Matthew 11:29

In *A Tree Full of Angels*, Macrina Wiederkehr refers to herself as "little great one."[1] This description aptly embodies humility because it admits to both her virtues and her limitations. Humility does not deny goodness, nor does it hide the less-than-honorable parts of self. When we see only the side of us that does not match up to our idea of saintliness, this is not humility but poor self-worth. Humility confesses mistakes, false judgments, and failures to act from our core goodness. We also enable this virtue when we acknowledge our talents and positive behaviors. Being humble includes asking for help when we prefer doing something by ourselves but cannot do it. Persons in recovery from addictions experience this every time they rely on their

Higher Power in order to cease using what destructs their lives.

We learn from Jesus how to be "gentle and humble in heart" by noticing how he refused to exaggerate his healing ability. We also see how he avoided putting himself down by not discounting that positive trait. While his gifts led to his being an exceptional teacher, he experienced humility when people remained unconvinced about his wisdom and refused to accept his teachings. Jesus lived this virtue by accepting his inability to change unjust systems that pressed people into poverty. Humility kept him from self-reproach. Jesus did not pretend to be anyone other than who he was.

Truthful Guide,
teach me how to be humble in heart,
to value that which is positive in myself
and also to acknowledge my shortcomings.
In consenting to the truth of who I truly am,
I do so with an unpretentious acceptance.

Today: I practice being humble in heart.

ONE WHO TRUSTS

And can any of you by worrying add a single hour to your span of life?

—Luke 12:25

Jesus witnessed the birds of the air as he walked from place to place. He observed in their freedom of flight a metaphor of how to approach life's inevitable stresses. From this observation, he expressed confidence in the Holy One's care. Jesus trusted his *Abba* regarding concerns that pressed hard against his life, but this did not diminish his emotional responses to these concerns. Jesus was still greatly disturbed about his friend's death, grew angry at the hypocrisy of religious leaders, and expressed frustration when the disciples failed to absorb what he hoped to teach them. Jesus felt these emotions, but this did not mean he lacked trust in the Holy One's care for him.

I sat in chapel one morning praying with this gospel passage when I heard a large *thunk* from a bird flying into one of the transparent windows. That certainly got my attention. After some pondering about the incident in relation to what Jesus taught, I concluded that confidence in the Creator does not mean that accidents and troubling events do not occur. Rather, his metaphor urges us to stop worrying about things that may never come to pass. The future is not ours to define or control. Like Jesus, we allow our human emotions to arise, but then we move through and beyond them into trust. The Holy One will be with us, no matter what happens.

Guardian of my life,
when disturbing situations come charging in,
they tend to evoke worry and create anxiety.
I will place my trust in your promised care,
even though I may feel tossed and turmoiled.
I will go on having confidence in your refuge.

Today: I entrust every worry I have into the Holy
One's care.

ONE WHO OBEYS

Then he went down with them and came to Nazareth, and was obedient to them.

—Luke 2:51

As a young student, I found myself sitting out recess on a bench—punishment for calling my teacher "an old rooster." I do not remember what she insisted I do, but obviously I resisted her instructions. As I've aged, I recognize the necessity of obedience as part of life. I've learned that obeying God is about listening to the Spirit's direction, often voiced through human suggestion or obligation. Obeying does not mean doing something without regard to my personal preference or a concern for others. Obedience consists of carefully and prayerfully discerning how best to be a person whose life reflects the virtues Jesus lived and taught.

Throughout his life, Jesus freely chose to be obedient to the will of his Father by setting aside his human need to have everything go his way. He stayed attentive to his inner guide and discerned how best to extend his love in service to others. In our life, obedience requires that we too open ourselves to the promptings of this divine guidance. If we develop the spiritual practice of pausing for daily discernment—reflecting on what stirs in our thoughts and feelings and where we let those movements take us—we more readily sense how we are to make good decisions. By watchful listening and seeking valuable counsel, we wisely use our ability to obey and serve.

Spirit of Wisdom,
when difficult requirements and obligations
come charging in boldly with their entreaties,
release what wants to stay unmovable in me.
Lead me in the direction that you most desire.
Loosen my strong will so I will choose wisely.

Today: I do something of worth that I would rather not do.

ONE WHO LOVES ENEMIES

Love your enemies, do good to those who hate you.
—Luke 6:27

Familiar persons or strangers may criticize unfairly, deliberately try to antagonize, shut me out of their life, or even wish me dead due to my beliefs, social position, nationality, or religion. When they do this, they act as an enemy. I have a choice when this happens. Even if someone considers me their foe, I do not have to return a similar response. People will only become my enemy if I deliberately wish to injure or hassle them. This benefits no one and tosses away the possibility of moving beyond antipathies.

How do we pray for those who oppose us? How can our battered hearts muster up a peace-generating posture? When Jesus taught, "Love your enemies," he could have said—as author James Martin, S.J., does—"See that person as God sees him or her."[2] This frees us to stand apart from our emotional and mental entanglements. We can give people who oppose us over to the Holy One without demanding they accept our viewpoints. This is what Jesus would expect of us. We may not experience a feeling of affection for people who combat us, but we can intentionally place them in care of the Divine with no strings attached. We do so not with smugness or superiority. Rather, we freely let go of treating them like they are an enemy.

Wide Heart of Love,
when I want to respond to people's hostility
by falling into the deadly enemy-making trap,
seat me beside you in the kingdom of love.
Help me to see that there beside you
also sit those who oppose and do not like me.

Today: I cleanse my heart of any desire to make
enemies.

One Who Is Perceptive

For he himself knew what was in everyone.
—John 2:25

How well I remember my nineteen-year-old self sitting across from the insightful college professor who asked me if I had thought of entering a religious community. I was aghast. How did she know? I kept that thought tightly secreted. No one knew. Yet she did. This insightful woman recognized qualities in myself that I wanted to deny or avoid. She saw more than a frightened, naïve student sitting before her. She knew who I could be if I gave my heart to it. That day I met the perceptive Christ in Lillian Wagner.

I imagine people felt that way whenever they experienced the penetrating gaze and inward observance of Jesus. He looked far into their hearts and perceived who they were at a hidden level, sensing qualities that others missed. His perception stemmed not only from the fullness of his divinity. This attribute also came from human intuition and a willingness to go inward to his own heart. In being reflective, Jesus perceived more readily, making connections and sorting out observations, thereby seeing himself and others more clearly. We may not be naturally perceptive, but we can learn to set aside our own agendas and be more present when we are with others. Reflective pauses lead us to arrive at truer conclusions. We sense what lies beneath the speech and appearance of others and support them by our insightful understanding.

Clear-hearted Holy One,
I desire to act with the grace of perception,
to view others more lucidly and justly.
Clear away misunderstandings that I develop.
Guide me to see beyond external appearances.
May I perceive the good in others, as you did.

Today: I look for more than what I see on the surface.

THIRD WEEK OF LENT

ONE WHO ENCOURAGES GROWTH

Those who drink of the water that I will give them will never be thirsty.

—John 4:14

When Jesus met the Samaritan woman at the well, she thirsted for more than water but did not know how to discover what would ease her longing. Moreover, she had been spiritually dehydrated for such a long time that she could no longer name that thirst. The Samaritan woman's unexpected conversation with Jesus drew forth from the well of her heart more than she ever thought possible. He offered her the gift of her true self, leading her to the heart's secret place and resurrecting the essential goodness she had forgotten. This awakening woman fought and mistrusted the freeing process until she finally accepted wholeheartedly what she truly desired. When this authentic love surfaced in her, she couldn't wait to tell the people of her village.

Like the Samaritan woman, we receive this gift when we are receptive and ready for it. I have been to the well, desiring something more than I was able to name but wanting it as much as a disoriented hiker in a desert aches for water. My efforts yielded sparse relief until grace came in unexpected forms—a wise mentor, a revealing dream, a touch of nature, the reception of a sacrament, and other life-giving sources that quenched my thirst.

We act like Jesus at the well when the Spirit in us listens compassionately to another person's dashed dreams until they are truly heard.

Encouraging Companion,
drop the measureless bucket of grace
into the well of my waiting heart.
Draw forth the virtues that live in me.
May every person who comes my way
find benefits from what my well contains.

Today: I listen to someone who thirsts to be heard.

ONE WHO HAS INTEGRITY

They were astonished at his teaching because he spoke with authority.

—Luke 4:32

Integrity comes from a word meaning "untouched, whole, entire, or complete," indicating that the person we believe ourselves to be actually matches our attitudes and the actions we undertake. The familiar phrase "walk your talk" perhaps best describes the essence of this virtue. Jesus spoke with an authority that revealed his integrity and truthfulness. His words did not come from a desire to have power over others or a need to manipulate them through his statements. Rather, his teaching and deeds proved effective because they originated from the core of his being. When Jesus spoke and acted, he came across as authentic, clear, and believable. He was genuinely himself. His power originated from the truth of his transparent existence.

When a lack of integrity forms like cataracts on our eyes, our verbal communication and the way we conduct ourselves gradually grow hazy. We no longer view our way of approaching life clearly. A spiritual blindness develops through debilitating habits. This nonawareness leads to harmful behaviors, such as a routine dishonesty, false criticism, and damaging jealousy. These behaviors accumulate until integrity becomes hidden behind the veil of hypocrisy. Integrity insists we speak to others with genuineness, not giving false assertions or speaking half-truths. Do our statements come from the depths of who we are? Does anything about our attitudes require removal so our attributes of goodness match what we say and do?

Authentic Teacher,
clear away any debris of hidden falseness
that has formed cataracts on my view of self.
I desire to see my harmful habits more clearly.
May I also have a better vision of the ways
that I already live as a person of clear integrity.

Today: My words and deeds match my truest self.

ONE WHO IS COMPASSIONATE

I have compassion for the crowd.

—Matthew 15:32

Hurting persons turned up everywhere Jesus went—hungry people, impoverished beggars, a widow burying her only son, a young man burdened with seizures, a woman shamed by the public, and a father desperate for his daughter to be healed. Jesus embraced with empathy these people and many more. He received their sorrow and distress with care. This compassionate approach required much from him. He was willing to keep a place in his heart for the suffering of others. Day after day he focused his attention on those around him, giving them the precious gift of his kindhearted presence. He set aside any desire to run from the pain-filled moans, desperate pleas, unpleasant odors, bodily wounds, and other distasteful aspects of those he served.

Rarely a day goes by without interacting with people who suffer, whether that be through the daily news, strangers we meet, or those we know personally. Sometimes we do not want to know or feel what another is going through, but we can still choose to be there in a caring way, because compassion is more than an emotion. This virtue involves empathy (allowing the hurt of another to reach our mind and heart) and taking action (being willing to do what we can to lessen the suffering). When we stand in solidarity with the hurting ones in our life and open our hearts to them, much will be required of us, as it was of Jesus.

Compassionate One,
open my eyes clearly enough to recognize
where suffering exists in the lives of others.
Open my heart deeply enough to activate
a sense of empathy and a willingness to care.
Open my hands wide enough to offer assistance.

Today: I respond compassionately to those who suffer.

ONE WHO OFFERS REST

Come to me, all you that are weary and are carrying
heavy burdens, and I will give you rest.

—Matthew 11:28

Remember how good your body feels after a revitalizing night's sleep? Jesus promises a similar restoration for our spirit. He experienced this support from his own sojourns during solitude and mountainside prayer. He does not imply that heavy burdens will be forever lifted, nor does he guarantee that he will magically deliver us from the interior invasions we tend to resist. Jesus does assure us that he will be there to lean on, to keep us from being overcome by life's weighty forces. Much depends on a small but significant word: "Come." If we are to experience this opportune reprieve from what drains us, we will approach the Source of our rest with a readiness to receive what is offered. Allowing space for personal renewal through stillness empowers us to become open and ready to welcome this supportive relief.

We can join in actualizing this promised respite by being present to weary people whose heavy burdens leach their strength and whose incessant trials shove out their serenity. We are a conduit of Christ's rest to these persons when we sit with them in surgery waiting rooms, listen to concerns that drain hope, lend helping hands to ease an overload of physical work, and give comfort when sorrow drags grieving spirits into isolation. Each of us has the ability to activate this beautiful quality of Jesus.

———————

Haven of rest,
you are balm for what wearies my spirit,
a comfort for that which troubles my soul.
Today I lean my heavy burdens and woes
on the promise of your unwavering presence.
I renew my trust in your unshakable peace.

Today: I provide rest for someone with a heavy burden.

ONE WHO AFFIRMS

Jesus said, "I tell you, not even in Israel have I found such faith."

—Luke 7:9

If you read the gospels with an eye for spoken affirmations, you will notice that Jesus easily praises others. He admires the centurion for his strong faith and marvels at the generosity of the woman who bathes his feet with her tears. He applauds Mary of Bethany for her willingness to listen and affirms the leper who returns to give thanks. He praises Nathaniel for being someone without deceit. Jesus obviously believed that affirmation had value not only as a catalyst for others to feel good about themselves but equally as a gift of supportive encouragement for enlivening their innate virtues.

True affirmation could be confused with false flattery. The latter arises from a variety of insincere motivations, including trying to get on the good side of someone, wanting to have a similar affirmation returned, or hoping to evasively alleviate a conflict that has arisen. Genuine praise sees with the eyes and heart of Jesus, believing in the good that resides in another. (Notice that Jesus did not comment on the clothes people wore or on their physical features. He praised their interior qualities.) Affirming others for who they are and how they act does not take a great deal of effort. It does, however, ask for thoughtfulness and genuine honesty. How often do we pause from our preoccupations and take time to affirm someone for how they manifest the goodness residing within them?

Voice of praise,
thank you for the encouragement I receive
when other people affirm my virtuous traits.
May I offer a similar gift to those around me,
confirming the innate goodness they possess.
Remind me to pause and speak words of praise.

Today: I affirm someone for a virtue they possess.

ONE WHO
MAINTAINS PEACE

[Jesus] said to the sea, "Peace! Be still!"

—Mark 4:39

Faith and peace go hand in hand. During the life-threatening storm at sea, the disciples had cause to be extremely frightened, yet Jesus questioned their lack of belief in his caring presence. He used the situation to stress maintaining a trusting approach in troubled circumstances. Jesus understood the importance of this from his own life. He had to go on believing in the worth of his ministry, even though what he desired for others appeared to be falling apart. The long nights spent in prayer enabled him to continue peacefully the chaotic journey he had undertaken. This same Calmer of hearts encourages us to have faith during our rough tempests. Peace doesn't ignore or deny the difficult things but instead retains equanimity during occurrences that appear hopeless. Faith gives us the courage not to give up and to trust that all will be well, no matter what happens.

We bring the calming presence of Christ to others by listening to their concerns when they are caught in turbulent tempests. We provide a safe shelter of welcome in the home of our heart, not judging their responses and apprehensions regarding their inner squalls. The presence of the peaceful Spirit moves though us, encouraging those in dismay to engender calmness rather than anxiety. While we may not be able to dispel their storms in the way Jesus did, our caring presence helps to prevent their boat of life from capsizing.

Calmer of hearts,
you steady my spirit when the storms of life
disturb and threaten to drown my peace.
When I am with others who are distraught,
may I bring the same unwavering presence
to calm the harsh tempests that menace them.

Today: I remain calm during the day's little or big storms.

ONE WHO FORGIVES

For if you forgive others their trespasses, your heavenly Father will also forgive you.

—Matthew 6:14

Move through one of the gospels and you will inevitably come across a passage where Jesus forgives someone or teaches on that topic. He not only speaks about this; he acts on it, absolving those who cause him pain. He does not harden his heart, make others apologize first, or hold grudges. When we are hurt by others, our first response might be a natural, human one of anger, hurt, or a desire for revenge. Being stabbed in the heart by another's vitriolic words and actions leaves a sharp, emotional gash. Our wounded spirits do not heal quickly. Old, painful memories rise up like bristly brushes. But eventually we face the question that leads to healing: "Will I forgive and love as Jesus has loved?"

Equally vital is our acceptance of forgiveness from someone else. Such a heavy weight lifts in knowing that the pardon being sought has been received. I recall a former parishioner apologizing to me for his rudeness from many years earlier. I did not remember anything about the incident, but I could tell by the sadness in his eyes that I needed to acknowledge what he was asking of me. I smiled warmly and replied, "Thank you. I appreciate your coming to tell me this." Instantly, the look on his face changed. I saw immense relief as tears welled in his eyes. How good it is to be forgiven.

Blessed Forgiver,
you know the old memories jabbing my heart,
the ones still in need of more prayerful attention.
You never give up on my ability to forgive.
You are there for me with unfaltering support,
no matter how long the absolving process takes.

Today: I move closer to forgiving as Jesus did.

FOURTH WEEK
OF LENT

ONE WHO IS PATIENT

While he was still far off, his father saw him . . . ; he ran and put his arms around him.

—Luke 15:20

How well we know the story of the wild and reckless son who took off with his inheritance, unmindful of the pain it caused those he left behind. With no concern for anyone else, the prodigal son's gluttonous focus on himself ended up ruining his life. The son fixated on what allowed him unmitigated indulgence, while his father focused on unconditional love, faithfully watching, believing, and waiting with perpetual hope for his child's return. This story contains a succinct example of how complete self-orientation precipitates personal disaster and how unconditional love leads to an open-hearted homecoming.

Jesus used this parable to teach about the forbearing love of God, who waits and waits for us. This patient One does not place all sorts of conditions on homecoming, never indicates, "I'll love you *if*," or "I'll love you *when*." This divine heart of reliable love simply embraces us when we choose to return, saying to all who act like the self-indulgent son, "You come back when you're ready. I'll leave the porchlight on." Jesus taught that we have a welcome waiting for us, no matter how long it takes to recognize the egocentricity that exhausts our integrity. When we remember how this patient Presence has welcomed us home, let it be an incentive for us to do the same for someone else who's been lost and awaits our embrace.

Patient Presence,
you wait, always ready to receive me anew
when I wander into my self-centeredness.
Thank you for keeping the porchlight on,
for assuring me of your hearty welcome.
May I readily offer this same kind of hospitality.

Today: I am patient with someone who is coming home.

ONE WHO LIVES GRATEFULLY

Then one of them, when he saw that he was healed, turned back . . . and thanked him.

—Luke 17:15–16

It occurs to me that Jesus valued gratitude from others as much as we do. His comment "Were not ten made clean? But the other nine, where are they?" tells me that the grateful leper's response meant something positive to Jesus (Lk 17:17). He also expressed his own thanks. After "the seventy returned with joy" from their mission of preaching and healing, he prayed in gratitude to his Father (Lk 10:17; see Lk 10:21). Before feeding the thousands on the hillside, he took the loaves and gave thanks, and again, at the Last Supper, when blessing the bread and cup (see Jn 6:11; Lk 22:17–19). Jesus also turned to grateful prayer after the stone covering the tomb of Lazarus was removed: "Father, I thank you for having heard me" (Jn 11:41).

Before I retire in the evening, I tuck the words of Psalm 23:6 into my heart: "Surely goodness and mercy shall follow me all the days of my life." These remarkable gifts not only follow me; they catch up with me every single day. Life moves swiftly, so I remind myself before going to sleep to cast a glance over the day to see what I find there. Inevitably, I brush a bit of debris aside. But hidden in those elements I find a lot that represents the precious benedictions of "goodness and mercy." If I look closely, I find these treasures strewn everywhere. I hold them to my heart with gratefulness.

Giver of gifts,
my heart opens wide with gratitude,
knowing my life is filled with abundance.
Even on tough days, if I look carefully,
I can always find something of worth within it.
Thus, I come to you with thanksgiving.

Today: I look for goodness and kindness and give thanks.

ONE WHO HEALS

[Jesus] said to him: "Do you want to be made well?"
—John 5:6

Everywhere he went Jesus engendered some type of healing. Twisted limbs on bodies straightened out. Wild spirits fled. Minds functioned normally again. Wounded people found hope and regained self-esteem. No wonder throngs of people pressed closely to be touched by him. The dictionary defines *healing* as "to free from injury or disease: to make sound or whole."[1] Sometimes healing takes a long time. It took the man by the Bethesda pool thirty-eight years.

Although people want to say yes to the question Jesus posed to this man, they do not always know they have need of healing. At age fifty, I left my regular work for two years of graduate study in psychology. I sensed a remote, inner voice whispering, "Pray for healing." I questioned that. I felt fine, inside and out. What needed to be made well? I went on to pray for healing, anyway. How astounded I was to discover during those years that parts of me did, indeed, need to be made well. I left graduate school with freedom from past engulfment in my own need for control, was healed from a push to be right, and became unchained from a driven concern to live up to people's expectations. The Spirit of Jesus touched my unhealthy self through the skilled care of a therapist and devoted teachers who restored my inner health. I learned that the Great Healer knows what needs be made whole and will provide healing if we are ready.

Tender Healer,
I come to the pool of my own Bethesda
trusting in the touch of your curative love.
Move within the depths of my being
and heal the remnants of past wounding
that linger and keep me from being whole.

Today: I am ready and receptive to receive
Christ's healing.

ONE WHO IS NONVIOLENT

Jesus said to Peter, "Put your sword back into its sheath."

—John 18:11

How can Jesus be considered nonviolent? Did he not call the Pharisees vipers and hypocrites and issue a statement saying he would bring division among households? There are several things to consider. The prevailing attitude of Jesus consisted of compassionate peacefulness, even though he did not deny that rifts might develop due to his teachings. We know that Jesus promoted justice and morality in both religious and human law. He did not endorse brutality, hatred, violent behavior, coarse language, or urge injury to anyone. On the contrary, Jesus constantly endeavored to heal body and spirit. Even when he knew crucifixion awaited him, he did not allow Peter to strike back.

When he stood before Pilate, Jesus accepted his fate rather than urging his followers to gather and wage a battle of destruction against those arranging to get him killed.

Being nonviolent may well be one of the most difficult virtues to put into practice. Who of us does not want to lash out and get back at those who enflame or mock us with their volatile words, damaging behavior, and hostile gestures? How hard it is to put away our swords of angry comments and the impulsive desire that others get what they deserve. Let us consider how our thoughts, speech, written messages, and actions contribute to sources of violence.

Source of nonviolence,
assist me in nurturing peacefulness
in my thoughts, words, and deeds.
Soften whatever hardens my heart.
I want to forego any movement within me
that might cause injury to another person.

Today: I search for ways that I can be nonviolent.

ONE WHO IS RESPECTFUL

You lack one thing; go, sell what you own, and give
the money to the poor . . . ; then come, follow me.
—Mark 10:21

When the rich man inquired what to do beyond keeping the basic commandments, his desire to grow spiritually touched Jesus, and he quickly became fond of
him. Jesus recognized the prosperous man's potential
for growth if he could cease being absorbed in his hoard
of material possessions. Jesus proposed a tough choice:
"Let go of what holds you back. Leave it behind and
follow me." This was too much for the inquirer, who
"was shocked and went away grieving" (Mk 10:22),
unable to accept what could have transformed his life.
Notice that Jesus did not harangue or berate the man's
decision by relentlessly trying to convince him that he
was making a big mistake. Jesus simply held out the

possibility for growth. When that choice was refused, Jesus did not nag or criticize. He understood that the man was not ready to give away what imprisoned his heart.

How much I have to learn from the way Jesus responded. When I deem it necessary to challenge someone to grow and they ignore the suggestion, I want to try harder, find another way to persuade them to change. This is my ego hard at work, not the Spirit moving through my being. It is not up to me to transform another person. I can suggest a possibility. Then I move on with respect, and leave the changing in God's hands.

Respectful Guide,
how often you have patiently waited for me
until I was ready to grow spiritually.
Ready my heart to listen to your suggestions
and to have the courage to accept and follow them.
I will forego my pushy efforts to change people.

Today: I examine how I go about trying to get
others to change.

ONE WHO GIVES GENEROUSLY

Give, and it will be given to you. . . . For the measure
you give will be the measure you get back.

—Luke 6:38

Generosity could have been Jesus' middle name. While
he never contributed a large financial donation or
bought expensive gifts for his friends, he gave liber-
ally from his nonmaterial resources. Jesus profusely
poured out his forgiveness, mercy, healing, and compassion. This lavish love contained more benefits than
most people could imagine. No wonder strangers were
drawn to Jesus. They noticed the richness of his generous spirit and realized that what he shared could make
a significant difference for what troubled them.

I learned a lot from my mother's aunt about giving to others without being overly cautious. Aunt Ida's
bank account held little, but her heart contained a vast

amount of hospitality and kindheartedness. As a child I noticed the way she cheerfully shared her home and meager food items with those of us who came to visit. Like the generosity of Jesus, my great-aunt went beyond what the law required. We too have the choice to give from our interior and exterior possessions, doing so either with restraint or with bounty. Questions arise: What do we find most difficult to share with others? What holds us back from giving what might benefit someone? What ordinarily motivates our giving? How liberal are we with our time, talents, and material possessions? Do we need to change anything in our lives in order to be more generous?

Abundant Gift-Giver,
you pour forth the treasures of your love
into both my interior and exterior life.
These gifts comfort, sustain, and enfold me.
I am assured that I have all that is necessary
in order to give my heart entirely to you.

Today: I give to others as generously as Jesus did.

ONE WHO CONVEYS POSITIVE ENERGY

But Jesus said, "Someone touched me; for I noticed that power had gone out from me."

—Luke 8:46

On the Feast of Our Lady of Guadalupe, I stood among crowds of people closely pressing against one another near the basilica in Mexico City. A button on my jacket got caught on the back of a man's loosely knitted sweater. I frantically tried to stop the unraveling and finally got the thread and button separated. I breathed a sigh of relief that he had not noticed. What a different story with the woman touching the hem of Jesus' robe in her desperate hope to be healed from twelve years of constant menstrual flow. As soon as her hand connected with the cloth, intense healing energy went forth from Jesus.

While we do not have the same amount of energy as Jesus, our beings contain our own dynamism. Much depends on whether we believe that we possess this and if we desire to share it. As we become more aware of those who suffer, we can deliberately gather the movement (energy) of love within us and send this forth to them. Not only theologians but also quantum physicists assure us that we have the ability to reach others in this way. Why not try this meditation? Close your eyes. Be in touch with the Source of love at the center of your soul. Then picture the person who hurts. Intentionally send this love forth to him or her.

Energizing Life,
thank you for the positive, restorative energy
that flows from your indwelling presence.
I unite with you in complete confidence,
assured of your transformative grace within me.
May I bring your healing love to those who suffer.

Today: I send forth the Source of love to someone in need.

FIFTH WEEK OF LENT

One Who Brings Freedom

And Jesus said, "Neither do I condemn you. Go your way, and from now on do not sin again."

—John 8:11

A woman was about to be stoned to death for adultery. Before the horrible killing could take place, Jesus arrived to challenge her accusers about their own transgressions. He saw the hypocrisy behind the stones they grasped. Every clenched rock intended to aim at her held the weight of their own sins. How quickly they must have dropped the heaviness in their hands, knowing Jesus accurately named the truth of their callous hearts. When Jesus turned to the woman being accused, he met a fragile human being caught in the net of her weakness and confusion. Instead of hurling harsh words of condemnation at her, Jesus spoke kindly and opened a way out.

He provides this same opportunity for us when we are caught in the mesh of our failings. We are not condemned. We are allowed freedom to mend our ways and start anew. When we activate this quality of Jesus in ourselves, we bring a merciful attitude toward those we prefer to denounce. We acknowledge injustice and other sinfulness, but we also look at the stones in our hearts and words, knowing they bear markers of our own wrongdoings. We allow for the possibility of a fresh start for everyone. Jesus gifted the woman caught in adultery with freedom. He also gives this to us. Surely we can extend the same to others.

————————————

Bringer of freedom,
as you beckon me with a merciful gaze,
I am well aware of how I have failed.
I want to unbind what holds me back from you
so that I can release my love more completely.
Thank you for approaching me so kindly.

Today: I pray that I will enlarge my heart of mercy.

ONE WHO
EMBODIES LIGHT

I am the light of the world. Whoever follows me . . .
will have the light of life.

—John 8:12

Why did Jesus choose light as a way to describe himself? He could have said, "I am the tree," or "I am the flow of the river," but instead he used light. I recall this when I'm sitting in my place of morning prayer with the dawn appearing beyond the wide windows. With the coming of daylight, revelation arrives with a view not perceived in darkness. Warmth reaches the earth with a drawing power that awakens life. *Light evokes life*. Like a tiny sprout requiring sunlight for its direction of growth, so does the Christ-light draw each person toward the development of their virtues.

Not only did Jesus indicate that *he* was the Light, but he urged those who followed him to believe *they* also radiated divine light: "You are the light of the world. . . . Let your light shine before others, so that they may see your good works" (Mt 5:14, 16). Jesus acknowledged people's inner goodness and counseled them to trust their potential. He offered guidance through parables and other teachings to help bring those qualities to fruition. For some of us, this reality of our being the "light of the world" requires more faith than does believing that Jesus embodies the fullness of divinity. Yet he insists that we are light-filled human beings. Each of us is meant to be the kind of radiant presence that evokes life, one that warms the hearts of others with our love.

Light of the world,
you illuminate and guide my daily path.
In my midnight hours of darkness,
you never let go of my trembling hand.
May I be a source of your revealing light
for others who are seeking to find their way.

Today: I radiate Christ's light wherever I am.

ONE WHO LIVES SIMPLY

> He ordered them to take nothing for their journey
> except a staff; no bread, no bag, no money in their
> belts.
>
> —Mark 6:8

How would Jesus choose to live simply in our consumer culture? In his public ministry, he appears to have had few material possessions. The gospels tell us he moved about unencumbered by baggage of any sort. We do not hear him asking for more than what he needs. We also read about Jesus encouraging his disciples to go freely and lightly in their travels, taking only the essentials with them. This meant they would be relying on the people they encountered to provide for their necessities. His directives also indicate that their hearts be centered on values deeper and longer-lasting than physical stuff.

When I walked the five-hundred-mile pilgrimage to Santiago, Spain, I carried all my belongings in a backpack. It was one of the most freeing experiences I have known. Ever since then, I find it easy and desirable to live simply. I do not want a lot of things. What remains difficult is my persistent urge to grab tightly certain nonmaterial items, such as my precious time and neatly arranged schedule. When I clutch these too firmly, it leads to my being overly fixated on myself. There are countless ways to live simply. Each of us decides on the how, depending on what prevents us from focusing on the most valuable and lasting treasure: a relationship with the Holy One.

Wayfarer of simplicity,
when I cling tightly to certain possessions,
they can take over my relationship with you.
Lead me to seek what is of greatest value,
so I continually give you my fullest love.
May I choose wisely what claims my heart.

Today: I let go of something that prevents me from loving well.

ONE WHO SPEAKS TRUTHFULLY

You will know the truth, and the truth will make you free.

—John 8:32

Authenticity rests at the center of Jesus' virtues. Dishonesty does not reside in his personal interactions or his lessons. Jesus sought truth and voiced it. He was honest to the core and spoke directly when someone questioned or challenged his mission. Not once did Jesus use deception to encourage others to think well of him or to lessen the antagonism of those who refused to accept his presence and message. The truth set Jesus free because he could let go of what others thought of him. He did not succumb to the ego's need of wanting to please everyone in order to be admired, nor did he inflate and exaggerate his obvious successes so he would look important.

Would that our society valued this virtue of truthfulness, to be willing to stand up for what is right and commendable. Instead, honesty has become corroded with deceitfulness, false excuses, sidestepping blame, and fabricated stories. It is difficult to decipher who is telling the truth and who is not. This applies not just to big issues but to smaller ones as well that progressively develop an established pattern of pretense. Think of how easy it is to devise an excuse for not attending a social function, to add negative comments to baseless rumors, or to cheat on financial matters. Each dishonesty of ours tears apart the moral fabric of civilization and undermines its ability to bring about good.

Spirit of truth,
sweep through my mind and heart.
Clear it from any tendency I may have
to use deceptiveness for my benefit.
I want to be aware of subtle dishonesty
so that my words and actions are genuine.

Today: I speak the truth in every situation.

ONE WHO PROMOTES JUSTICE

The Spirit of the Lord . . . has sent me . . . to let the oppressed go free.

—Luke 4:18

Toward the beginning of his Galilean ministry, Jesus stood in the synagogue and spoke the words of the prophet Isaiah: "The Spirit of the Lord is upon me . . . to bring good news to the poor . . . to proclaim release to the captives and recovery of sight to the blind, to let the oppressed go free." After this, he confirmed his ministerial purpose by saying: "Today this scripture has been fulfilled"—indicating that the text applied to himself (Lk 4:18, 21; see Is 61:1). Jesus went on to live this inauguration speech to the utmost. He spoke frequently of the necessity to amend wrongs against oppressed people, to see to their well-being and bring about justice. He went directly to those pushed to the margins of society and challenged his disciples to do the same: to tend to people suffering from poverty, rejection, and inequality.

Gregory Boyle, S.J., has spent many years in Los Angeles working with a rehabilitation program for former gang members. In speaking about this program, Boyle encourages his listeners, as Jesus did, to be with those who have been pushed aside and led to believe they have little significance or worth. Let us join in listening to disregarded persons like these and be their advocate when society ignores their plight and refuses to hear their voice. We can befriend someone who appears different from ourselves, support those lacking basic rights, and contact legislators on their behalf.

Motivator of justice,
hurry me toward the margins of society,
to where you firmly stood with compassion
for those lacking justice and recognition.
I move beyond my fear and lack of motivation
because I truly want to follow in your footsteps.

Today: I evaluate how I promote justice.

ONE WHO
VALUES NATURE

He spat on the ground and made mud with the saliva and spread the mud on the man's eyes.

—John 9:6

Fig trees, camels, seeds, birds, water, salt, flowers—how many elements of nature Jesus connected to his teachings. He even used mud to heal a blind man's eyes. Jesus lived close to the earth. He did not travel by auto or public transportation. His feet moved him upon the blessedness of the ground beneath him. When he entered cities and villages, he breathed the air and felt the wind sweep across his face. He prayed and rested on the hillsides, walked along the seashore, and voyaged upon the water. Jesus touched the planet's life with reverence and appreciation. He found deeper meaning among its simple gifts, lessons that arose from mindfully living among these natural resources.

What do we experience when we encounter the natural world? Our physical senses, such as sight, hearing, and touch, have a marvelous ability to awaken our spirit. When we pause to be with nature by using these senses—hearing the melody of a bird song, seeing the hued colors of vegetation, feeling the strength of stone, tasting a sweet strawberry, or smelling the air after a fresh rain—we open our inner senses to receive insights, as Jesus did. When the exterior world of nature informs our interior world in this way, gratitude, wonder, and a sense of unity with all that exists may well spring forth to gift us.

Creator of life,
stimulate and alert my external senses
when they grow dull with inattention.
Guide me to notice Earth's inspiring teachings.
I will move among the gifts of nature as you did
and discover their hidden meaning for my life.

Today: I pay attention to something in nature.

ONE WHO COMFORTS

When [Jesus] saw her, he had compassion for her and said to her, "Do not weep."

—Luke 7:13

A widow overcome with her loss accompanies the funeral procession of her only son. Jesus sees her as he walks nearby and responds with empathy to the immensity of her sadness. He realizes that not only has she lost a beloved child, but she also will have no financial support because she is a widow. He follows the natural impulse of his heart and reaches out to her, reviving the son and giving him back to his mother. All it took to relieve her pain was the movement of his compassion and a few words: "Young man, I say to you, rise!" (Lk 7:14).

We rarely receive back something precious we have lost, but we are often able to benefit from divine compassion, as did the widow of Nain. When my father died suddenly, I was forty years old. His death shattered my joy. Not long after this misfortune, a friend sent a sympathy card that brought me much-needed comfort. The cover of the card portrayed a lamb carefully cradled with two strong hands, obviously those of the Good Shepherd. I felt consoled in knowing that I was being held with a similar kind of embrace. The compassion of the Holy One found me through the empathy of my friend's simple, caring gesture. Sometimes the most ordinary expressions of compassion bring about the most extra-ordinary gifts of comfort.

Heart of comfort,
time and again you wrap your tenderness
around my confusion and unhappiness.
Remind me, when I hesitate or forget,
that I can bring your comforting presence
to the hurting people who enter my life.

Today: I comfort a person who experiences hurt.

Sixth Week of Lent
(Holy Week)

ONE WHO IS COURAGEOUS

Then he entered Jerusalem.

—Mark 11:11

Jesus decided to go to Jerusalem even though his death seemed imminent. He could have done otherwise, fleeing to another country and hiding out in some secret place, gathering his supporters to fight the enemies, or even going so far as to soften or cease his powerful teachings regarding societal and personal transformation. Instead, Jesus chose to step into the impending peril, to be true to the voice of the Spirit nudging him forward, despite the danger. This took a tremendous amount of courage.

Suffering ought not be something we seek and venerate. By itself, there is nothing romantic or holy about suffering. But when it arrives unexpectedly or comes as part of our decision to live in a Christlike manner, suffering acts as a catalyst for reliance on divine strength. Suffering can expand our compassion. Courage enables us to enter into and meet our own Jerusalems, those situations that elicit physical, emotional, mental, or spiritual pain. We walk with Jesus into Jerusalem when we choose to enter into circumstances such as being a caregiver day after day with no relief or leisure in sight, standing up to an injustice that results in personal rejection by those we thought to be our advocates and friends, supporting someone in fragile recovery from an addiction, or any other situation that we know will demand a lot from us.

Courageous Christ,
on that day when you rode upon the donkey,
processing amid the cheering palm-wavers,
surely your courage struggled to remain intact.
I will face my entrance into unavoidable suffering
and draw strength from your ability to accept it.

Today: I draw courage from how Jesus entered
Jerusalem.

ONE WHO RECEIVES GRACIOUSLY

> Mary took a pound of costly perfume . . . anointed Jesus' feet, and wiped them with her hair.
>
> —John 12:3

Six days before the Passover, Jesus went to his friends' home in Bethany. There Mary knelt at his feet and anointed them with an expensive, fragrant oil used for anointing bodies of the deceased. Not only did Mary lavish this oil on his feet, but she also used her long hair to wipe them dry. This tender, intimate gesture of devotion must have moved Jesus deeply. He did not protest Mary's kindness by saying, "Oh, you don't need to do that," "No sense wasting that expensive stuff on me," "I should be doing that for you," or "Save it until I'm dead." Instead, he humbly and willingly received this precious gift, praising Mary for her loving attentiveness.

Imagine someone doing for you what Mary did for Jesus. I would feel awkward and embarrassed. Along with a lot of other people, I prefer to reach out rather than receive in. When we are the receptors of another's generosity, especially if it involves something materially expensive or requires a considerable amount of their time, we can feel vulnerable, assume we are unworthy of accepting their generosity, or doubt our own inner strength when we receive from someone who appears to be stronger or have more to give than we do. We might feel uncomfortable, put upon, or even guilty because we are unable to return the favor. Jesus teaches us in his reception of Mary's lavishness that receiving is as important as giving.

Gracious Recipient,
you humbly received the outpouring of Mary's love.
When I resist, push aside, or outright refuse
to accept the assistance or attention of someone,
grant me the grace to be open and receptive,
gracious enough to consent to what is offered.

Today: I thank someone for a kindness given to
me.

ONE WHO UNDERSTANDS

Jesus answered [Peter], ". . . Before the cock crows, you will have denied me three times."

—John 13:38

Peter was prone to overstatement and bragging. At times, he fell into the trap of being impulsive, head-strong, and too sure of himself. He forgot to preface his responses with reflective pauses, relying instead on his exaggerated self-importance. Jesus experienced these flaws in his friend. He knew Peter could bend under the pressure of fear, that he might easily say or do something he would regret later on. Knowing this, however, did not eliminate disappointment and pain for Jesus when Peter acted this way and denied that he ever knew him. But Jesus understood. He believed Peter was more than his flaws and failings. He loved him and did not give up on this imperfect disciple.

With age and wisdom, it becomes apparent to me that everyone exists with certain character flaws and shortcomings. As much as I would like this reality to be different, there are no unblemished, perfect people, including myself. Knowing this, I understand when others do not always match up to how I hope them to be. While I do not condone or accept the wrong they may have done, my compassion understands how it could happen. I want to go on loving them, just as Jesus did with Peter. He focused on the goodness dwelling within his headstrong disciple and encouraged the best of Peter to come forth. What a valuable example for all of us.

God of second chances,
teach me to stop poking at my deficiencies
and to cease expecting others to be perfect.
May I remember the life-altering question
you spoke to your disciple who failed you:
"Do you love me?"

Today: I accept people as they are, not as I want
them to be.

ONE WHO IS VULNERABLE

They paid [Judas] thirty pieces of silver. And from that moment he began to look for an opportunity to betray him.

—Matthew 26:15–16

A line from C. S. Lewis's book *The Four Loves* has stayed with me since my twenties: "To love at all is to be vulnerable."[1] Lewis implies that when someone invests in a relationship, there exists the possibility of betrayal. Jesus trusted Judas and expected him to be faithful when he became his disciple. I picture the two of them walking in the countryside, sharing countless meals, a kind of brotherhood developing between them. This makes the betrayal by Judas all the more devastating. In choosing to love Judas, Jesus risked being wounded. What a terrible blow to have this friend sell his very life to those who wished him dead.

Anyone who has given their trust and then experienced betrayal or rejection can identify with this piercing heart-wound. More than once I have known the pain of my invested loyalty being flung aside by someone I valued. Each time I wanted to close the door to my inner realm and let no one have access. But that was not the way of Jesus, and it cannot be my way either if I am to grow in the qualities he embodied, which include being vulnerable. When the wise investments of our love are betrayed, we cannot be so guarded and self-protected that we cease allowing others to venture forth into our heart.

Vulnerable Mentor,
no matter how severely your invested love
was trampled on by another's disloyalty,
you did not turn toward hatred or revenge.
Instead, you kept the door of your heart open.
I will do likewise and choose to be vulnerable.

Today: I unite my heart with my Vulnerable Mentor.

ONE WHO SERVES

Then [Jesus] poured water into a basin and began to wash the disciples' feet and to wipe them with the towel.

—John 13:5

Jesus already served in numerous ways by ministering to the physical and spiritual needs of others, but nothing compared to this menial task. What was it like for him to get down on his knees and wash those dirty, well-traveled feet? We know from scripture that Peter did not like seeing Jesus in this position and protested loudly that he was not about to let Jesus wash *his* feet. Peter couldn't envision this amazing leader and healer doing this lowly task. Jesus still went ahead and washed Peter's feet, showing the disciples that loving service takes many forms, including a common chore such as cleaning someone's feet. Jesus did not exhibit ego-led authoritarian power or use domination over those who received from his leadership. His choice of foot-washing speaks loudly to the message of serving with a humble posture of mind and heart.

Not long ago, I went to a Friday-night-in-Lent fish fry hosted by members of the Knights of Columbus. I watched with admiration how these men of varied professions donned aprons and spent the evening in the kitchen absorbing the stinky odor of fish while they gave themselves to the jobs of meal preparation for several hundred hungry folks. Each man cooked food and tended tables with a graciousness any host would be proud of. These servants demonstrated dedication, humility, and generosity, putting into practice the foot-washing that Jesus did for his disciples.

Dedicated Servant,
there are certain times when I am called
to perform menial tasks that I dislike.
Wipe away any superiority or self-importance
that clings to my resistance in serving others.
I want to approach work in the way you did.

Today: I accomplish my tasks with a spirit of
humble service.

Good Friday

ONE WHO SURRENDERS ALL

Then Jesus, crying with a loud voice, said, "Father, into your hands I commend my spirit."

—Luke 23:46

The hour had come—beaten and stripped not only of his clothes but also of his mission, success, and future plans—Jesus' work was finished, whether he wanted it to be or not. He who had given totally of himself for the sake of others now hung dying on the limbs of a tree. He felt abandoned. What sounded like despair and utter failure would eventually be remembered by his disciples as a tremendous moment of yielded love. The desolation of Jesus on the Cross would become a powerful symbol of complete surrender to an infinite Love, whose affectionate, compassionate heart embraces all.

Endless opportunities emerge throughout our lives, insisting that we let go of what holds us back from completely giving ourselves to the Holy One. This surrender involves a willingness to cease pushing to have only what we can control. As much as we would like it to be so, we do not have the ability to manage everything by ourselves. This reality leads to our having to make a consequential choice: to release ourselves trustingly to God's love or to claw our way further into resistance against life's inevitable crosses. Author Cynthia Bourgeault notes that many revered writers on the topic of spirituality have come to this conclusion: "All along it has been surrender carrying them home" to the heart of God.[2] Will we also let *surrender* carry us home?

Surrendered Son,
your cry of agony and abandonment
echoes in the chambers of my heart.
The final surrender of your entire being
into the waiting embrace of your Abba
inspires me also to let go and yield to Love.

Today: I join with Jesus in his surrender.

Holy Saturday

ONE WHO WAITS IN DARKNESS

Then Joseph bought a linen cloth, and taking down
the body, wrapped it . . . and laid it in a tomb.

—Mark 15:46

In *Stations of the Light*, Mary Ford-Grabowsky refers
to the empty tomb of Holy Saturday as "a site of new
life," a place of "dark, silent fertility."[3] While no one
can say what actually took place for the spirit of Jesus
while his body lay in the grave, scripture does indicate
a powerful change between his death on Friday and
his reappearance on Sunday. This time of his interment
represents a chrysalis-like, transformative stage of quiet obscurity, one that necessarily precedes the unfold-
ing of a hope-filled future.

Holy Saturday invites us to consider the in-between periods of our lives when the reality of painful loss clings tightly and the possibility of moving on

eludes us. We too have our Holy Saturday experiences—similar to physical death but repeated throughout life—when the grayness of our little "deaths" entombs us in a silent vagueness. During these periods, we find ourselves waiting for something to happen, hoping things will change for the better as we restlessly seek inner harmony. Like Jesus, we hover somewhere between the bleakness of a Good Friday and the brilliant light of an Easter Sunday. Similar to a butterfly in a chrysalis completing its preparation, we wait with faith-filled expectation of new grace arriving. We have hope that our day of emergence will come and, with it, a revival of joy.

Hidden One,
you entered the dark space of in-between,
where the gestating grace of the Holy One
empowered an amazing transformation.
Your silent entombment teaches me to be patient
when my own chrysalis-time requires waiting.

Today: I recall how my entombments helped me
to grow.

ONE WHO IS
A LOVING MENTOR

Then they told what had happened on the road,
and how he had been made known to them in the
breaking of the bread.

—Luke 24:35

"Without Easter, we wouldn't know Jesus. If his story
had ended with his crucifixion, he most likely would
have been forgotten. . . . There would have been no
abiding community to remember and give meaning
to his life,"[1] writes Marcus Borg and John Dominic
Crossan. The resurrected Christ brought joyful con-
firmation not only of his divinity but of his presence
as a loving mentor and faithful friend. His risen presence assured the disciples that he did not leave them
orphaned. Jesus returned to bring their discouraged
hearts his gift of abiding peace. He continues to bring
this gift to us.

We traveled through Lent reflecting on attributes of
our Teacher and Friend of our soul, Jesus of Nazareth.

Now we go forth into the Galilee of our lives to cultivate and activate those virtues in more comprehensive ways. When we enliven the qualities of Jesus through how we live, we become witnesses of his teachings. The familiar saying "actions speak louder than words" truly applies to our Christian journey. The virtues of our Mentor of love live on through us.

The two disciples on the road to Emmaus recognized Jesus in his action of breaking bread. As we move on, let us ask ourselves this question: How will people on the road of life recognize the risen Christ in us?

―――――――――――

Risen Christ,
your presence abides within and around me.
As I continue to make my way through life,
may all that I am and all that I do each day
demonstrate and reflect your radiant goodness.
I rejoice in the renewed kinship I have with you.

Today: I celebrate the risen Christ's abiding
presence.

The world and time
and all created by God
are eastering and rising up
to life again.
The universe and all of us
are the result
of unbearable tenderness,
and we are laced and threaded
with everlasting life
that cannot and will not
ever be undone.
Hope surrounds
and delight stalks our every step,
because Love still reigns
and seeks us out
no matter where we hide or live.

—Megan McKenna,
The New Stations of the Cross[1]

QUESTIONS FOR REFLECTION

These questions can be either for your personal reflection or for use in a faith-sharing group. They are meant to be considered once a week during Lent. Begin by choosing one of the prayers from the week. Pray it aloud. Follow this with a few minutes of quiet time to recall the past week of prayer with *Jesus, Friend of My Soul*. Then proceed with the following and any other questions you deem suitable to the faith-sharing conversation or to your personal reflection.

As you look back over the past week, consider the following questions:

1. Which reflections most inspired and encouraged you? What aspect of Jesus most caught your attention?

2. Which day presented the greatest challenge? What stirred in you as you pondered that particular reflection?

3. What virtue or quality from this week do you find easiest to accept and activate? Give an example of when this quality has been expressed through you.

Is there a person, other than Jesus, who has been a mentor and example for you in living this quality?

4. Which virtue or positive aspect is most difficult for you to activate? What causes this to be challenging for you?

5. If you were to choose an image or symbol to describe the past week of praying with the qualities of Jesus, what would you choose and why?

6. How would you describe your Lenten journey thus far?

7. Is there anything else about the reflections that is calling for your attention?

Close each time of reflection by praying aloud one of the other prayers from the week.

During the final time of reflection during or after Holy Week, create a time of quiet to respond to this question: How would you summarize your experience of praying with *Jesus, Friend of My Soul* during the Lenten season?

NOTES

Introduction

1. St. Symeon the New Theologian, quoted in *Give Us This Day*, February 6, 2019, 76–77.

2. Frederick Buechner, *The Faces of Jesus* (New York: Simon and Schuster, 1974), ix.

3. John O'Donohue and John Quinn, *Walking in Wonder: Eternal Wisdom for a Modern World* (New York: Convergent Books, 2018), 7.

4. Beatrice Bruteau, *The Easter Mysteries* (New York: Crossroad, 2017), 49.

First Week of Lent

1. Francis Weller, *The Wild Edge of Sorrow: Rituals of Renewal and the Sacred Work of Grief* (Berkeley, CA: North Atlantic Books, 2015), 7.

2. *Merriam-Webster*, s.v. "reconcile," accessed June 20, 2019, https://www.merriam-webster.com/dictionary/reconciling.

Second Week of Lent

1. Macrina Wiederkehr, *A Tree Full of Angels: Seeing the Holy in the Ordinary* (San Francisco: HarperOne, 2018), 1.

2. James Martin, S.J., *Building a Bridge: How the Catholic Church and LGBT Community Can Enter into a Relationship of Respect, Compassion, and Sensitivity* (San Francisco: HarperOne, 2018), 98.

Fourth Week of Lent

1. *Merriam-Webster*, s.v. "heal," accessed June 21, 2019, https://www.merriam-webster.com/dictionary/healing.

Sixth Week of Lent (Holy Week)

1. C. S. Lewis, *The Four Loves* (San Francisco: HarperOne, 2017), 155.

2. Cynthia Bourgeault, *The Heart of Centering Prayer: Nondual Christianity in Theory and Practice* (Boulder, CO: Shambhala, 2016), 75.

3. Mary Ford-Grabowsky, *Stations of the Light: Renewing the Ancient Christian Practice of the Via Lucis as a Spiritual Tool for Today* (New York: Image, 2007), 5.

Easter Sunday

1. Marcus Borg and John Dominic Crossan, *The Last Week: What the Gospels Really Teach about Jesus's Final Days in Jerusalem* (San Francisco: HarperOne, 2007), 190.

Concluding Quote

1. Megan McKenna, *The New Stations of the Cross: The Way of the Cross According to Scripture* (New York: Image Books, Doubleday, 2003), 121.

Joyce Rupp is well known for her work as a writer, spiritual midwife, international retreat leader, and conference speaker. She is the author of numerous bestselling books, including *Praying Our Goodbyes*, *Open the Door*, and *Fragments of Your Ancient Name*. Her 2018 book, *Boundless Compassion*, won awards from the Association of Catholic Publishers and from the Catholic Press Association. Her books *Fly While You Still Have Wings* and *Anchors for the Soul* also have earned CPA awards. Rupp is a member of the Servite (Servants of Mary) community

joycerupp.com